ABOUT THE BIBLE

ABOUT THE BIBLE

Short Answers to Big Questions

TERENCE E. FRETHEIM

Augsburg

MINNEAPOLIS

ABOUT THE BIBLE
Short Answers to Big Questions

The following chapters originally appeared as Terence E. Fretheim's "About the Bible" column in *Lutheran Woman Today:* Chap. 1: Sept. 1996 *LWT.* Chap. 2: Oct. 1996 *LWT.* Chap. 3: Nov. 1996 *LWT.* Chap. 4: Dec. 1996 *LWT.* Chap. 5: Jan. 1997 *LWT.* Chap. 6: Feb. 1997 *LWT.* Chap. 7: March 1997 *LWT.* Chap. 8: April 1997 *LWT.* Chap. 9: May 1997 *LWT.* Chap. 10: June 1997 *LWT.* Chap. 11: July/Aug. 1997 *LWT.* Chap. 12: Sept. 1997 *LWT.* Chap. 13: Jan./Feb. 1998 *LWT.* Chap. 14: Oct. 1997 *LWT.* Chap. 15: Nov. 1997 *LWT.* Chap. 16: Dec. 1997 *LWT.* Chap. 17: March 1998 *LWT.* Chap. 18: April 1998 *LWT.* Chap. 19: May 1998 *LWT.* Chap. 20: June 1998 *LWT.* Chap. 23: July/Aug. 1998 *LWT.*

Chap. 21 originally appeared as an article in the March 1999 *Lutheran Woman Today.* Chap. 22 appears here for the first time.

Cover design by Mike Mihelich.
Cover image courtesy of PhotoDisc, Inc.
Cover photo courtesy of Luther Seminary.
Text design by James Satter.

Library of Congress Cataloging-in-Publication Data

Fretheim, Terence E.
    About the Bible : short answers to big questions / Terence E. Fretheim
        p.   cm.
    Includes bibliographical references (p.).
    ISBN 0-8066-3867-2 (alk. paper)
    1. Bible—Introduction. 2. Bible—History. I. Title.
BS475.2.F73 1999
220.6'1—dc21
                                         99-17453
                                                CIP

Manufactured in the U.S.A.   AF 10-38672

03   02   01   00   99   1   2   3   4   5   6   7   8   9   10

Contents

1

Questions Anyone?

THE PRESS HAS RECENTLY REPORTED a sharp increase in Bible sales across the United States. The reasons for this increase are disputed. But people both within the church and outside of the church seem to have an increasing number of questions about the Bible. Perhaps now, more than at any recent time, people are less hesitant to ask questions about the Bible. Exploring these questions together is a wonderful opportunity to witness to the faith.

Suppose a friend asks you, "What is the Bible, anyway?" How would you respond? You might say, simply, "The Bible is the Word of God." Good! That's a fine beginning. But what if your friend presses you with other questions, like these:

1. Why do Roman Catholics have more books in their Bible than Protestants do?

2. Why do Jews have a Bible with the same books as the Protestant Old Testament, but in a different order?

3. Can more books be added to the Bible?

4. Did Jesus have a Bible? Did the authors of the New Testament books?

5. In what language(s) was the Bible written?

6. What translation of the Bible do you use? Why? Why are various translations of the Bible often different from one another? Are some translations better than others?

7. When was the Bible written?

8. Who wrote the Bible?

9. What types of literature are found in the Bible?

10. Did everything reported in the Bible actually happen? Is everything in the Bible to be taken, or interpreted, literally?

11. When you say the Bible is true, what do you mean? Are there differences of fact or opinion within the Bible?

12. What do you mean when you say that the Bible is "inspired"? Just how does God speak to people?

13. What do you mean when you say that the Bible has "authority"? Does the New Testament have more authority for Christians than the Old Testament?

14. Does everything in the Bible apply to Christian faith and life today? Is everything in the Bible equally important for Christians today?

15. What role should the Bible play in our everyday lives? How should we use the Bible to explore today's issues?

16. How do personal life experiences affect how you read and interpret the Bible?

17. Why do Christians often interpret the Bible differently? How should we best talk about our differences?

18. Are there religious matters that the Bible does not talk about—and questions that the Bible doesn't answer?

19. Can Bible texts have more than one meaning? Or, is there one original meaning for every text?

20. What are some good methods or tools for studying the Bible?

In the chapters ahead, we will look at questions like these. Perhaps adult forums, women's circles, or other small groups will want to use these chapters to kick off discussions. Make it work for you as the Holy Spirit guides you.

LEARNING—A POWERFUL WITNESS

All too often for Christians, Bible piety is not matched by Bible literacy. That is, we revere the Bible highly, but we often don't really know very much about it. As Christians who hold the Bible in high esteem, we will want to learn as much about it as we can. We will want to ask our questions freely. And we will want to be able to talk helpfully to people who ask their own questions about the Bible. Our response may be an important witness to them.

Think about it: If we are not able to say very much about the Bible, others may wonder why we hold it so dear. It may even seem, in some odd way, that we are embarrassed by the Bible! Learning more about the Bible can help us to interpret it in more mature ways. It can help us come to informed and stimulating conclusions about the meaning of many things in the Bible. And it will enable us to witness more thoughtfully and powerfully to the faith we confess.

It's important to remember that there are not always concrete answers to questions about the Bible. But, even without definitive answers, questions are sometimes the most helpful avenues to insight. Living with questions over time is important because they keep us thinking about matters that are key to our faith. Even more, living with questions will mean we can better recognize answers if and when they come our way.

Discussion Questions

1. What has been your experience (in the church or elsewhere) when asking questions about the Bible or about the Bible's content?

2. Which of these questions are you most curious about or troubled by? Why?

2

How Did Your Bible Grow?

THE WORD *BIBLE* COMES FROM a Greek word that means "books." One helpful way to describe the Bible is to say it is a collection of books. These books were written by many different authors over the course of more than 1,000 years. So, while the Bible is a book, it is also many books. You could say the Bible is a book of books.

Protestant Bibles contain sixty-six books. While the Bibles of all Christians contain these books, the Bibles of some church bodies have several additional Old Testament books. We will look at this topic in the next chapter.

The Bible is more than simply a collection of books. The word *Bible* (or *scriptures*) also designates those books that are authoritative for the faith and life of the Christian community. Another word used to refer to this list of books is *canon*; these books are called the canonical books.

How were all these books gathered together to form our Bible? It's a complicated story, and we don't know all the details. We do know, however, that these books were not recognized as part of the "Bible" when they were first written. Authors did not set out to write books to be included in the Bible. Indeed, these authors would no doubt be surprised to see what has happened to their books!

We also know that the canon did not come into being all at once—it was a gradual process. The Bible "grew" in stages over the course of several centuries. Two main phases in this process can be identified.

First, individual books were used throughout the years in teaching and in worship. This happened both in the Jewish community (for those books that became the Hebrew Bible, what Christians call the Old Testament) and in the Christian community (for those books that became the New Testament). As these books were used, they became more and more authoritative.

Second, at various times and places these books were officially recognized as canonical—that is, part of the Bible—but we do not know exactly how or when.

THE OLD TESTAMENT

The books of the Old Testament were written over the course of many centuries, with the last book written around the year 165 B.C. Although how and when these books became canonical is uncertain, three major developments can be noted:

1. *The Law*—Genesis through Deuteronomy—was first recognized as Holy Scripture, probably by 400 B.C. or so. This may be the "book of the law of Moses" publicly recognized in Nehemiah 8:1-18.

2. *The Prophets*—Joshua through 2 Kings (except Ruth), Isaiah, Jeremiah, Ezekiel, and the twelve minor prophets—were next recognized as Scripture, probably by 200 B.C.

3. *The Writings*—the other Old Testament books. This section remained undefined until 90 to 100 A.D., more than sixty years after Jesus' death. About that time, the Jewish community in Palestine placed its seal of approval on the present thirty-nine books of the Hebrew Bible. This development recognized the stature that these books, one by one, had attained during earlier years. The Christian church was not bound by Jewish decisions, of course, and this third section of the canon remained loosely defined for Christians for many years (more on this in the next chapter).

THE NEW TESTAMENT

The New Testament books were written over the course of about fifty years (50 to 100 A.D.). These books were written for several reasons. First, early Christians recognized the need to preserve the memory of Jesus' life and teachings. Also, as the number of Christian converts increased throughout the Mediterranean world, it became important to provide instruction regarding the essentials of the Christian faith. These books enjoyed widespread use in the churches in the years after they were written.

How and when these books became canonical for Christians is uncertain. Certainly by 200 A.D. the letters of Paul and the Gospels—and probably several other books—were considered canonical. The status of a few books varied for a time, depending on the needs and interests of Christians in various areas. The New Testament as we now know it was probably not firmly in place until about 350 A.D.

Over the next few chapters, we'll look at some of the implications of the way this "book of books" became the Bible as we know it.

Discussion Questions

1.   What does it mean to say that the Bible "grew"?

2.   In what ways does this chapter challenge your understanding of the Bible?

3

Why Is Your Bible Different from Mine?

NOT ALL BIBLES ARE THE SAME. This truth can sometimes be confusing for Bible readers. What are these differences—and how did they come about? Sorting through these differences can help us to better understand our Bible.

One difference can be seen in the various available translations of the Bible. We will talk about translations in chapters 5 through 7.

A second difference relates to the number of books in the Bible. While all Christians have the same twenty-seven New Testament books, they disagree regarding the number of books in the Old Testament canon—that list of authoritative books we discussed in the previous chapter. While Protestant and Jewish Bibles have thirty-nine Old Testament books, the Bible used by Roman Catholic and Eastern Orthodox Christians include the thirty-nine books and additional writings. The interesting result is that while Protestants and Jews agree on the number of Old Testament books, the majority of Christians in the world have a larger Old Testament.

The Roman Catholic Old Testament contains seven extra books, plus additions to the books of Esther and Daniel. These books and additions were written during the three centuries before Jesus. They help us fill out the story of the Jewish community during this time. The books of Tobit and Judith are placed between Nehemiah and Esther, while 1 and 2 Maccabees follow Esther. The books of Wisdom (or the Wisdom of Solomon) and Sirach or Ecclesiasticus (not to be confused with Ecclesiastes) are similar to the book of Proverbs; they have been placed after the Song of Songs. The book of Baruch, because of its association with Jeremiah, follows Lamentations.

The Eastern Orthodox churches also include these additional books. Some Orthodox Bibles contain still other books. For example, the Greek Orthodox church includes the Prayer of Manasseh, Psalm 151, 1 Esdras, and 3 Maccabees, with 4 Maccabees in an appendix.

Sometimes these extra books are called the Apocrypha, a word meaning "secret, hidden," that is, not intended for public reading. But that term is really an inexact description. And so, these days the extra books are usually referred to as the deutero-canonical books, that is, a "second canon" (in Greek, *deutero* means second). Some Protestant Bibles print these extra writings as a block between the Old and New Testaments. This follows the practice of Martin Luther, who considered these books "not equal to the Sacred Scriptures, but useful and good for reading."

A third difference in Bibles is the way in which Old Testament books are arranged. The books in all Christian Bibles appear in the same order. They fall into four blocks: law (Genesis through Deuteronomy); historical books (Joshua through Esther); psalms and wisdom (Job through Song of Songs); and the prophets.

The Hebrew Bible, however, from which our Old Testament is translated, places the books in a different order. The Hebrew Bible arranges these books into three sections: the Law, the Prophets, and the Writings.

These differences are part of the complex history of how our Bible came to be the way it now is. We looked at some of these matters in the last chapter; here are a few more details.

In the third century before Jesus, the Hebrew Bible began to be translated into Greek. This came about to fill the need of an increasing number of Jews who lived outside of Palestine (especially in Egypt) and spoke only Greek. This translation, called the Septuagint, took several centuries to complete. For unknown reasons, its ordering of the books differed from the Hebrew Bible; the Septuagint also included deutero-canonical books, but their number was never fixed.

Jesus and some early Christians may have used the Hebrew Bible in the form it had during their time (see Luke 24:44, where the risen Christ speaks of "the law of Moses, the prophets, and the psalms"). However, the authors of the New Testament books usually quoted from the Septuagint. Indeed, this Greek text was the Bible used by most early Christians. Hence, Christian Bibles have used its book order.

The status of the extra books remained somewhat fluid in early Christian history. Still, most Christian writers used an Old Testament that included extra books until the time of the Reformation (sixteenth century). At that time, the Reformers chose the shorter Old Testament, while the Roman Catholics decided (in 1546) for the larger canon. In the next chapter, we'll look at the question: "Can books be added to the Bible?"

Discussion Questions

1. Have you ever discussed differences in the structure of the Bible with someone of a different faith? How significant were these differences?

2. If you have never read from a deutero-canonical book, find a Bible that includes them and read from it. Start with Judith 8-16 or Susanna. If you have read from a deutero-canonical book, what's your favorite story from that book?

4

Can Books Be Added to the Bible?

SOME VERY IMPORTANT religious books have been written over the years since the Bible was completed. One thinks of St. Augustine's *Confessions* and Martin Luther's Small Catechism. They have probably shaped the faith and the lives of Christians in ways more profound than some biblical books (for example, Song of Songs or Jude). Why don't we add them to the Bible?

Or, what if a previously unknown book by Jeremiah or letter of Paul were discovered in a cave somewhere in the Middle East? Could it be added to our Bible? If so, how might the process work? These questions prompt several observations.

1. The inclusion, or exclusion, of books that form the Bible could have been different from what it was. The Holy Spirit was at work in the hearts and minds of those who were involved in the "growing" of the Bible. But it may be that one or more books were lost along the way. During biblical times the books now in our Bible consisted of separate scrolls rather than a book that could be held in one hand. In such a "loose-leaf" system, books could more easily be added or removed or misplaced. Because God chose to act through human beings, one or more books might have been included or excluded than would have been the case had God acted alone.

2. Generally speaking, history has long since decided the issue regarding the books in the Bible. The Bible exists as a body of literature, and we have to come to terms with it as it stands. With regard to the sixty-six books, no disagreement exists among Christians. A difference among Christians does continue regarding a few Old Testament books (see last chapter). But this difference is an issue centered on those specific books—they have a special status among the books that might be considered for inclusion in the Bible because of their common use in the churches for centuries. At the same time, it is agreed that they do not contribute anything distinctive to the Christian faith. How this difference might be resolved is uncertain at the present time, but it shows that the precise boundaries of the Bible are not essential to the church's teaching and self-understanding.

3. The Lutheran confessional writings (and the constitution of the Evangelical Lutheran Church in America) speak of the Scriptures as canonical, but they do not list the books one by one. Nor does the Bible itself contain such a list (although modern publishers often put in a table of contents). So, *theoretically*, the way is open to include other books in the Bible, although, *practically*, the canon is now closed.

Yet, if another letter of Paul or a book by Jeremiah were discovered, their inclusion in the Bible could be considered. But the decision-making process would take a long time. The book(s) would have to be used in the churches for an extended period of time, as was the case with all biblical books at various times in the past. If, in time, they gained authoritative status in the eyes of many people, the church could raise the issue of their inclusion in the Bible.

4. Why do we give the canonical books of the Bible a special place that other books do not have? One factor to consider is the closeness of the biblical books to the decisive events at the heart of our faith, particularly God's act in Jesus Christ. These events provided a context for decision-making on the status of books— a context that is no longer available to us. There can never be a *primary* witness to these events again.

5. Earlier does not necessarily mean *better*, however, so other factors have to be taken into account. To speak of the canon is to speak of the fundamental source for Christian self-identity. These books are confessed to be a sufficient and adequate basis for establishing and maintaining such an identity. The Christian turns to these books to ask what the essence of the faith was—and still properly is—and what it means to be a person of faith:

As a person of faith, I am Sarah and Abraham, recipient of God's promises and called to bring that promise to others.

As a person of faith, I am also Hagar the outsider, the divorced mother with child, the homeless woman, yet recipient of God's promises, too.

I am Jacob, that rascal and cheat, yet nevertheless loved by God and chosen to further God's purposes in the world.

I am Joseph, and have all kinds of problems with my brothers, but I have been placed in a position of power and entrusted by God to seek the well-being of others.

I am the speaker of Psalms, who at times cries out from the depths for grace and mercy, but also knows that the Lord is my shepherd and I shall not want.

I am the prophet who is called not only to speak out against the injustices I see around me, but also to speak the promises of God and to testify to their fulfillment in Jesus Christ.

These books identify who I am as a person of faith. They speak my language. In them I hear God's word of judgment and grace. In these books I find a home. I cannot demonstrate their truthfulness in any conclusive way, but I have found them to ring true with my own experience and that of many others.

Discussion Questions

1. Which book of the Bible do you feel is the most important? Why?

2. If you had to shorten the Bible by one book, which one would you choose? Why?

5

Why Are Bible Translations So Different?

PART 1

STRICTLY SPEAKING, most of you reading this chapter do not have a Bible in your homes. Most of you have one or more versions (translations) of the Bible—originally written in Hebrew (most of the Old Testament), Aramaic (a few segments of the Old Testament), and Greek (the New Testament). Now, of course, you *do* have a Bible. But it is very important to remember that you have a Bible *translation*. In this chapter and in the next two chapters, we'll explore why translations are often so different.

We sometimes forget that the printing press was not invented until the fifteenth century. Before then, the Bible was copied by hand by Jewish (the Old Testament) and Christian scribes. Today we have no originals of any biblical book, only copies of copies. Several thousand of these copies (manuscripts) of the Bible (or parts of it) still exist today, but most of them were discovered only in the last 150 years. These manuscripts often differ from one another. In fact, there are tens of thousands of differences among them (called "variant readings").

Why so many differences? For one thing, many scribes worked independently in various places in the Middle East. And they didn't have telephones or fax machines to compare notes! Also, scribes, no matter how skilled, made mistakes. Think of the long, tedious hours it took to copy the Bible by hand—and without ballpoint pens or paper as we know it (animal skins were common)! When one thinks of how "typos" find their way even into printed books, it is remarkable that the differences are as minor as they usually are.

Mistakes arose most often because the scribes did not see or hear accurately. They skipped over (or repeated) letters or words, or even entire lines. Or, when one scribe read the text and several scribes copied what they heard, they heard differently, especially when words were similar in sound.

Later scribes at times spotted such mistakes and sought to correct them, perhaps on the basis of memory, or perhaps on the basis of a still different manuscript. Perhaps the scribes *thought* they detected a mistake or wanted to clarify a word or phrase, and took it upon themselves to "correct" the text. And so, in time, differing Hebrew and Greek manuscripts became available among Jews and in different parts of the church.

Translations of the Bible began to be made already during biblical times so that people could read the Bible in their own tongue. For example, the Jews began translating the Old Testament into Greek in the third century B.C. (the Septuagint). Christians began translating the Bible into Latin in the third century A.D. and in time this became the translation used in the church for more than 1,000 years (it was called the Vulgate). These translators did not all work from the same Hebrew and Greek manuscripts. Also, as we shall see in the next chapter, translating is not an exact science. And so, just as there are different English translations today, there were different Greek and Latin translations in circulation.

Christian scribes copied the entire Bible through the years in Greek or Latin. For centuries, however, only Jews handed down the Old Testament in the original Hebrew. Until recently, the oldest of these Hebrew manuscripts dated from the ninth and tenth centuries A.D. (older copies were destroyed as new ones were made). They have now been supplemented by manuscripts found about fifty years ago in caves in the Dead Sea area (especially near a place called Qumran). These manuscripts—more than 190 of them, most in fragments—date from the period of 250 B.C. to 135 A.D. Modern translators of the Old Testament work from these and other Hebrew manuscripts. Christians are thus heavily dependent upon centuries of careful Jewish scribal work for the Old Testament we have today.

Scholars have been working for years trying to determine the most original text of the Bible. The ever-new discovery of differing manuscripts has made their work more complex. They sort out the various manuscripts, note their differences, seek to discern the mistakes, compare them with the various older translations, and try to restore the original text.

Scholars do not always agree on details, and this makes for some of the differences we see in modern translations. But this detailed work, carried out by highly skilled people, has made it possible for us to be confident that the Bible we have today is very close to the original. For this work we should all be most thankful.

English translations first began to appear in the fourteenth century. We will look at these in the next chapter.

Discussion Questions

1. Why are Bible translations so different? Compare Genesis 1:1-3 in three different translations. Which is your favorite? Why? (See pages 27 and 28 for a list of translations.)

2. Choose a chapter of the Bible to read in your favorite translation. Read that same chapter in another translation. Are there any places where different translations of the same word expand your understanding?

6

Why Are Bible Translations So Different?

PART 2

ENGLISH TRANSLATIONS began to appear in the fourteenth century. The King James Version (KJV), published in 1611 and sponsored by King James I of England, soon became the authorized version for English-speaking Protestants and remained so for more than 300 years. The Douay-Rheims Version (1610) had a comparable status for Roman Catholics.

Today, however, the situation is quite different. More than fifty English translations of the New Testament have appeared since 1950! Why so many? Some reasons are good, for example, to update the language. Other reasons are less admirable, such as competition among publishing houses to reap the profits of Bible sales.

The most common recent English translations include the following:

1. The Revised Standard (RSV, 1952). This revision of the King James Version by American scholars was sponsored by the

National Council of Churches of Christ. The New Revised Standard Version (NRSV, 1989) is a major revision of the RSV.

2. The Contemporary English Version (CEV, 1995) was sponsored by the American Bible Society.

3. The New English Bible (NEB, 1970) was translated by British scholars for British readers. It was revised in 1989 and is known as the Revised English Bible (REB).

4. The New International Version (NIV, 1978) was initiated by evangelical churches and sponsored by the New York International Bible Society.

5. The Today's English Version (TEV, 1976; also known as the Good News Bible) was sponsored by the American Bible Society.

6. The Jerusalem Bible (JB, 1966) was developed under Roman Catholic auspices in Jerusalem, and it was revised in 1985 as the New Jerusalem Bible (NJB).

7. The New American Bible (NAB, 1970), by American Roman Catholic scholars, is authorized for Catholic readers.

8. The New Jewish Publication Society Bible (NJPS), completed in 1982, is sponsored by the Jewish Publication Society of America. Of course, it consists only of Old Testament books.

9. The Living Bible Paraphrased (LBP), was completed in 1971 by Kenneth N. Taylor.

Translators are concerned about two basic matters: accuracy and clarity. They seek to be faithful to the text while writing in clear and contemporary English. Beyond these common goals, many factors come into play, giving rise to many differences.

QUESTIONS TO ASK OF TRANSLATIONS

In this chapter we consider three questions to ask of any translation. Read the preface of your Bible to get answers to these and other questions.

1. What translation principles have been followed? Translating is not an exact science. No translation of the original Greek and Hebrew can be completely literal and still make sense to contemporary readers. The result is that every translation is an interpretation. That is, the point of view of the translators will shape the translation, often unintentionally.

Some translations, such as the NRSV and the NIV, have more literal, word-for-word translation. The basic principle of the NRSV is this: "As literal as possible, as free as necessary." Other translations, such as the Today's English Version, have a meaning-for-meaning translation. Still others, like the Living Bible, are paraphrases. The paraphrases are less literal, freer attempts to help the average reader immediately understand every word. Naturally, the less literal the translation is, the more likely the translation will reflect the perspective of the translators.

Look at these texts from Hosea as translated in the NRSV and TEV:

(4:19) "A wind has wrapped them in its wings" (NRSV). "They will be carried away as by the wind" (TEV).

(12:1)"Ephraim herds the wind, and pursues the east wind all day long" (NRSV). "Everything that the people of Israel do from morning to night is useless and destructive" (TEV).

Chances are you find the TEV easier to understand than the more literal NRSV. But what you gain in quickness you lose in depth. The image of the wind in the NRSV, for example, makes you stop and ponder the meaning. It is likely that, once you've thought about the wind for a while, more than one possible meaning will occur to you and the image (and the text!) will stick with you longer.

2. Is the translation the work of an individual or a committee? Most translations are the work of committees, but occasionally this is not the case. For example, the Living Bible is the work of one person, and his personal point of view (for example, he is a Baptist) is more evident. This can be seen in 1 Peter 3:21: "Baptism . . . now saves you" (in NRSV) compared to "In baptism we show that we have been saved" (in LBP). Committee translations are less affected by individual preferences.

3. Who are the sponsors and what is the makeup of the translation committee? Remember that translators have different points of view. The NRSV committee, for example, was made up of both female and male scholars who came from all major Protestant denominations (and which included Roman Catholic and Jewish representatives). The presence of women no doubt made a difference in some of its translations (see the next chapter). The NIV committee, for instance, was influenced by the perspectives of evangelical churches. One difference the latter makes may be seen in Psalm 2 where "Anointed One," "King," and "Son" are capitalized so as to make the connection with Jesus more evident.

In the next chapter, we will look at other factors that account for differences among translations.

Discussion Questions

1.   Read the preface to the Bible you normally read and note the membership of the committee (or the person) responsible for the translation.

2.   According to the preface of your Bible, what translation principles have been followed?

7

Why Are Bible Translations So Different?

PART 3

Eɴɢʟɪsʜ ʙɪʙʟᴇ ᴛʀᴀɴsʟᴀᴛɪᴏɴs are different for many reasons. We looked at some of those reasons in the last chapter when we highlighted eight English translations. Here are some other reasons why translations often differ. (See the box on the next page for the key to translation abbreviations.)

1. Gaps often exist in a text, and translators fill in the meaning with different words. Some translators may think a gap exists, while others do not. Take Jesus' word in Matthew 10:29 on sparrows. A literal translation would be: "Not one of them will fall to the ground apart from your Father," as in the NRSV. But several translators think something is missing or needs to be clarified, and therefore they add a word. So the RSV adds "without your Father's *will* "; the NIV reads "the *will* of your Father"; the NAB renders this "without your Father's *knowledge*"; and the LBP reads "without your Father *knowing* it." It makes a big difference how you translate this text! Without the added word, the text simply says that God is present with "sparrows" when they die. The additions suggest that every sparrow's death is part of God's will.

2.   The English language has changed over time. Take these differences in Philippians 4:14: "Notwithstanding ye have well done, that ye did communicate with my affliction" (KJV) and "In any case, it was kind of you to share my distress" (NRSV).

In other instances, new meanings of English words must be avoided. Psalm 50:9 (RSV) reads, "I will accept no bull from your house." One can see why the NRSV chose to read, "I will not accept a bull from your house."

Many translations now have changed the words *man* and *men* when they refer to women as well. For example, the NRSV uses "humankind" in Genesis 1:26-27 because it more accurately translates the original Hebrew word. The Greek word translated as "brethren" in the RSV often refers to all church members, so the NRSV correctly translates this as "brothers and sisters" in Galatians 1:11 and elsewhere. A similar example is to use the word "children" rather than "sons" (see Romans 8:19).

3.   Older and better manuscripts of the Bible recently have been discovered, and this has resulted in many changes. For example,

KJV	=	King James Version
LBP	=	Living Bible Paraphrase
NAB	=	New American Bible
NIV	=	New International Version
NRSV	=	New Revised Standard Version
RSV	=	Revised Standard Version

1 Samuel 10:27 is a much longer verse in the NRSV than in most translations because the NRSV follows the text of a recently discovered Dead Sea manuscript. Other translations may now make the same change.

Mark 16 is a much shorter chapter in the NRSV because, as the NIV states in an editorial preface to verse 9 and following, "The two most reliable early manuscripts do not have Mark 1: 9-20." Translations handle this problem differently, but the NRSV puts two different endings in brackets, with additional material in a footnote.

4. We now know more about Bible times and the biblical languages than we used to. For example, the KJV translated a Hebrew word several times as "unicorn" (see Job 39:9), only guessing what the word meant. A similar word was found in other ancient texts meaning "wild ox," and all modern translations now use the wild ox translation.

Or, the familiar Isaiah 53:4: "Surely he hath borne our griefs, and carried our sorrows" (KJV) is now (despite Handel's *Messiah*!) more correctly translated as "Surely he has borne our infirmities and carried our diseases" (NRSV).

5. Some biblical books are more difficult to translate. This may be because the grammar is difficult, the vocabulary rare, or the manuscripts are not in good condition. Such factors make for greater difficulties—and more disagreement—for translators. Job is one such difficult book. Look at the familiar Job 19:25-27 and all the footnotes (in NRSV), one of which tells us the "meaning of Heb[rew] of this verse uncertain." Yet we now know, again despite the *Messiah*, that there are no "worms"—as the KJV reads—in Job 19:26!

6. Disagreements exist among scholars for various reasons. Take Jeremiah 9:10. The NRSV has God commanding the prophet: "Take up weeping and wailing for the mountains, and a lamentation for the pastures of the wilderness." A footnote tells you, however, that for some reason NRSV has followed the translation of the Greek (Gr) and the Syriac (Syr) rather than the Hebrew. The Hebrew has God saying a more remarkable thing: "I [God] will take up weeping and wailing." The NIV—more correctly, I think—follows the original Hebrew, and then we understand the verse to mean that *God suffers* when the environment is destroyed.

New translations or revisions will continue to appear regularly as language changes and translation problems are resolved. So Bibles will continue to be very different. Many Bible editions have notes and study aids to inform you of some of these issues. The HarperCollins Study Bible (NRSV) is one of the best. Using multiple translations has its drawbacks. For example, when no one version is common to the church, not everyone uses the same translation for study, reflection, or memorization. On the other hand, using different Bible translations may help us understand the Bible better. As we delve into texts, comparing different translations can give us greater insight into God's word.

Discussion Questions

1. Compare 1 Samuel 10:27 in the NRSV to the same verse in any other Bible. What are the differences? Why do these differences exist?

2. Compare Mark 16 in two or more Bibles. How are they different? Why?

8

How Is the Bible Like the Sunday Paper?

THE SUNDAY PAPER contains various types of literature: news reports, editorials, feature articles, advice columns, comics, perhaps even a recipe or two. As you move from one type to another, you unconsciously adjust how you read. For example, you read a news report differently than you read an editorial or a movie review.

In fact, you probably know the sections of the paper so well that you can say something about the contents of each before you begin. Our knowledge of the kinds of literature in a newspaper increases our understanding.

We often forget that the Bible also consists of different types of literature. Learning to recognize these differences will help us to read and understand the Bible.

The two basic types of literature in the Bible are poetry and prose. You usually can tell the difference by the way in which the type is set up on the page. For example, look at the book of Job. The first two chapters are prose, chapter 3 begins a long section of poetry that continues through chapter 42, verse 6, after which the book concludes with prose. The book of Psalms is poetry; most of the book of Exodus is prose (but note chapter 15). The Gospel of Luke is mostly prose but has some poetry, especially in chapters 1 through 4.

Having noted this basic difference between prose and poetry, you can then make further distinctions within each category.

PROSE

The Bible contains various types of prose; among them are prayers (Genesis 32:9-12), letters (Galatians), parables (Luke 15), miracle stories (Mark 2:1-12), laws (Exodus 21), confessions of faith (Deuteronomy 26:5-9), and genealogies (Genesis 5).

POETRY

The Bible also contains various types of poetry, such as psalms, proverbs, songs (1 Samuel 2:1-10; Luke 1:46-55), blessings (Deuteronomy 33), and prophetic oracles (Hosea 11). Some of these types of poetry can be subdivided. For example, there are various types of psalms, such as hymns of praise (Psalm 100), songs of thanksgiving (Psalm 30), individual laments (Psalm 22), and community laments (Psalm 44).

IDENTIFYING TYPES OF LITERATURE

One basic question to ask when reading the Bible is: "What type of literature am I reading?" The answer will often influence how you read.

Sometimes the Bible will identify the type of literature. For example, Jesus tells us in Luke 15:3 that what follows is a parable, the parable of the lost sheep. Sometimes, however, the Bible leaves it up to the reader to identify the literary type. For example, the parables in Luke 15:8-10, Luke 15:11-32, and 2 Samuel 12:1-6 are not named as such. We recognize these texts as parables from knowing other examples of parables.

Remember that all types of literature can be used to speak the truth. So even though parables are a type of fictional literature, they are profoundly true.

Sometimes when a Bible passage does not tell us the literary type, it is difficult to identify what it is, and Bible readers will not always agree. For example, how would you identify the story about the trees in Judges 9:8-15? Some readers would say it is a parable. Others, noting that the chief characters of the story are trees, would call it a fable. In either case, the passage speaks the truth, even though we know the trees did not actually talk with one another!

Sometimes identifying a passage gets even trickier. Take Isaiah 5:1-7. Verse 1 says that what follows is a love song. But the prophet here seems to be telling a parable of judgment, much like the parable in which Nathan subtly indicts David for his actions with Bathsheba (see 2 Samuel 12:1-12). Verse 7 tells us the vineyard is not really a vineyard but the people of Israel. This means that the beloved who is the owner of the vineyard is actually God. The grapes that God expected are justice or righteousness, and the wild grapes that grew are bloodshed or the cry of people. Perhaps this passage is called a love song to entice the reader to read carefully.

Often you can identify the literary types in the Bible by repeated words or phrases, or by the outlines they follow. We will take a look at this in the next chapter.

Discussion Questions

1.   Answer the question in the title of this chapter: "How is your Bible like the Sunday paper?"

2.   Read your Bible at two or three different places. Ask yourself what type of literature you are reading.

9

How Are Some Psalms Similar?

In THE LAST CHAPTER, we examined how the Bible is filled with different types of literature. Prose and poetry are the two basic types. In this chapter we look at one type of poetry—the psalm.

Most psalms are found in the book of Psalms, but a few psalms are found in other books. For example, Hezekiah sings a psalm of thanksgiving after recovering from his sickness (Isaiah 38:9-20). Jonah sings this type of psalm after being saved from drowning by a fish (Jonah 2:1-9). Songs of thanksgiving are found throughout the book of Psalms, for example, Psalms 30, 32, 34, and 66.

Often you can identify the different psalm types by repeated words or common outlines. We examine two types of psalms from this perspective: hymns of praise and laments of the individual.

HYMNS OF PRAISE

These hymns express praise to God for all that God has done. At the same time, they are words about God, witnessing to God's great deeds before other people. A hymn of praise typically begins with a call to worship God; continues with a reason for worshiping God, signaled by the word *for;* and ends with a concluding praise of God. Let's look at Psalm 117 as an example.

PSALM 117

[1] Praise the LORD, all you nations!
Extol him, all you people!

The call to people to worship God (verse 1).

[2] For great is his steadfast love
toward us,
and the faithfulness of the
LORD endures forever.

The reason for worshiping God. Note the signal word "for" is there (verse 2a).

Praise the LORD.

Concluding praise of God (verse 2b). "Praise the LORD" is "hallelujah" in Hebrew.

Now turn to Psalm 100. Here the pattern varies a little. The people are twice called to worship God (100:1-2,4), and each call to worship is followed by the reason (100:3,5). No concluding word of praise is used.

Psalm 47 is similar (see also Psalm 95:1-7). The call to worship is repeated (47:1,6), as is the reason (47:2,7). The reason is expanded in this psalm (47:3-4,8-9). Then comes the concluding word of praise: "He is highly exalted." Another variation can be seen in Psalm 150, which contains mostly repeated calls to worship, ending with "Praise the Lord!" (Hallelujah!)

LAMENTS OF THE INDIVIDUAL

These psalms are prayers to God in a time of distress, such as sickness and troubles with other people. Again, you can identify this psalm type by the use of certain words ("How long") and a common outline. Nearly fifty psalms fall into this category. It is the most common type of psalm. Laments of the individual often include an invocation or cry to God for help, a petition or request to God to change the situation, reasons why God should act on the psalmist's behalf, a statement of trust or confidence in God, and the assurance of being heard by God. (See Psalm 13 on the next page.) This outline is followed by other laments in a general way. Sometimes the order varies and elements are repeated, just as in real life.

Turn to Psalm 142. The psalmist cries to God for help (142:1-2), expresses trust in God (142:3a), laments about her own suffering (142:3b-4), petitions God for help (142:5-6), says why she wants help (142:7a), and concludes with assurance (142:7b).

Psalm 55 is a more complicated lament, prayed by one who has been betrayed. The psalmist cries and petitions God for help (55:1-2a); describes her trouble and wants to escape (55:2b-8); petitions God for help again (55:9a,15), interspersed by a fuller description of suffering, especially betrayal (55:9b-14); voices confidence in God (55:16-19); returns to betrayal (55:20-21); and expresses certainty of being heard (55:23). Verse 22 may be a remembrance of what another believer has counseled her to do in such a time of trouble.

Jesus prays one of the lament psalms (Psalm 22) from the cross. The psalmist cries to God and complains (22:1-2), expresses trust in God (22:3-5), describes the suffering (22:6-8), returns to trust (22:9-10), petitions God (22:11), returns to

PSALM 13

¹ How long, O LORD? Will you
forget me forever?
How long will you hide your
face from me?

Invocation or cry to the Lord for help
("O LORD").
(Note the repeated use of the phrase
"How long.")

² How long must I bear pain in
my soul,
and have sorrow in my heart
all day long?
How long shall my enemy be
exalted over me?

Lament or complaint
(verses 1-2).

³ Consider and answer me,
O LORD my God!
Give light to my eyes, or I will
sleep the sleep of death,
⁴ and my enemy will say, "I have
prevailed";
my foes will rejoice because I
am shaken.

Petition or request to God for help
(verse 3).

Reasons why God should help
(verses 3-4).

⁵ But I trusted in your steadfast
love;
my heart shall rejoice in your
salvation.

Statement of trust
(verse 5a).
Assurance of being heard
(verses 5b).

⁶ I will sing to the LORD,
because he has dealt
bountifully with me.

Vow to praise God
(verse 6).

describing the suffering (22:12-18), and petitions God once again (22:19-21a). The psalmist concludes with an extensive word of assurance that God will rescue him and he will respond by praising God's name to others, who will also experience God's salvation (22:21b-31).

Jesus teaches us by this example that we have a wonderful resource in the psalms of lament for expressing our deepest needs and concerns to God.

Discussion Questions

1. Note the basic outline of Psalm 117. Turn to Psalm 47 and 95:1-7 and note how this outline is also present there.

2. Note the basic outline of Psalm 13. Turn to Psalms 55 and 142. Notice how this outline is also present there.

10

Why Do Metaphors Matter?

SHOULD WE INTERPRET the Bible literally? Sometimes, yes; sometimes, no. It depends on how words are used. Words may be used figuratively. Our common sense usually tells us when this is so, as with the "eye" of a needle (Mark 10:25) or the "branches" of a river (Isaiah 19:6). When Israel is called "stiff-necked" (2 Chronicles 30:8), this refers to a refusal to yield themselves to God, not the condition of their neck muscles. A good general rule: Interpret the text literally, unless there is good reason not to do so.

There is often good reason. For example, the Bible often uses hyperbole, or purposeful exaggeration. A mother uses hyperbole when she says to her child, "I've told you a *million* times to clean your room!" When Jesus says that "it is easier for a camel to go through the eye of a needle than for someone who is rich to enter the kingdom of God" (Mark 10:25), he uses overstatement. Similarly, when he says in Luke 6:41, "Why do you see the speck in your neighbor's eye, but do not notice the log in your own eye?" Also, when in Matthew 5:29 Jesus says, "If your right eye causes you to sin, tear it out and throw it away."

Another type of nonliteral speech is a metaphor. Jesus is the lamb of God (John 1:29). Or, God is a rock (Psalm 18:31).

Common sense tells us that Jesus is not literally a young sheep, nor is God a rock. A metaphor uses something more familiar (lamb, rock) to help us understand something that is less familiar (Jesus, God).

While these metaphors are not to be interpreted literally, they still convey truth. In order to discern the truth of a metaphor, however, we need to ask where the point of comparison lies. For example, in what ways is God *like* a rock and in what ways is God *not like* a rock? What do you think? We might say that God is like a rock because God is a sure foundation against the waves of life, but God is not like a rock because God is not hard or lifeless. You may have come up with even better ideas; there is no single answer.

A simile is a way of comparing much like a metaphor, only it explicitly uses the words *as* or *like*. For example, the righteous are *like* trees planted by streams of water (Psalm 1:3; see also Psalm 52:8; and 92:12-14) or God is as a father and has compassion for his children (Psalm 103:13). In these cases, the text gives us the point of comparison. As trees draw on life-giving water, so the righteous meditate on the law of God; God has compassion as fathers have. Yet, the righteous are *not like* trees in some ways, and God is *not like* a father in some ways.

Metaphors and similes are different ways of saying much the same thing. So, people are "like" grass (Psalm 103:15), and they "are" grass (Isaiah 50:6). Or, God "is" father of orphans (Psalm 68:5), and God is "as" a compassionate father (Psalm 103:13). In either case, our task is to discern the point(s) of comparison.

Sometimes these figures of speech can be more complex and their points less obvious. What does it mean to say that God is "like maggots" to Israel (Hosea 5:12)? What do you think? Use your imagination and your knowledge of maggots! Perhaps it means that God in judgment, like maggots, eats away only the diseased parts of the person. In most ways, God is *not like* maggots!

What does it mean that family unity is "like the precious oil on the head, running down upon the beard, on the beard of Aaron, running down over the collar of his robes" (Psalm 133: 1-2)? What do you think? Perhaps it means that the oil used for anointing the priest is like family unity in that it leaves a pleasant fragrance or spills over into all areas of life. It probably does not mean that family unity is messy or greasy!

What does it mean when Isaiah 64:8 says that "we are the clay, and you are our potter"? Where is the point of comparison? Does it mean that God has control over people as potters do with their clay? Does it mean that if the clay is spoiled in some way, it is God's fault (see Jeremiah 18:4)? Or, does it mean simply that "we are all the work of your hand," as Isaiah 64:8 suggests?

In the next chapter, we will take a look at the great variety of metaphors the Bible uses to speak of God.

Discussion Questions

1. How does hyperbole help you to understand Matthew 5:29?

2. In Deuteronomy 32:10-12, how is God both like an eagle and unlike an eagle?

3. How is God like and unlike a mother in Isaiah 42:14?

11

Does God Have Eyes and Ears?

IN THE LAST CHAPTER we looked at metaphors—words drawn from everyday life to describe what is less familiar. We saw that these words do not describe God literally; we have to look for the point of comparison. For example, at what point is God like a rock, and at what point is God not like a rock? The point of comparison is not always clear. There is no single answer. This chapter continues the discussion. Words from almost every sphere of life are used to speak of God.

1. The world of nature. God is depicted as fire (Hebrews 12:29), the morning dew (Hosea 14:5), an eagle (Deuteronomy 32: 11-12), and even maggots (Hosea 5:12), as we noted in the last chapter.

2. Social and political life. God is described as a king, a judge, a friend. God is "the friend of my youth" (Jeremiah 3:4; also see Psalm 25:14), and Jesus calls the disciples his friends (John 15:15).

3. Family. God is portrayed as a husband, a father, a mother. For example, in Isaiah 66:13, God comforts the people like a

48

mother. In Isaiah 42:14 the suffering of God is likened to a woman's pains in childbirth (see Deuteronomy 32:18).

4. *Human vocations.* God is shepherd, teacher, seamstress, midwife, physician, potter, metalworker, guard, warrior, farmer, even thief (Revelation 3:3). For example, in Psalm 139:13, God is imaged as a seamstress who "knit me together in my mother's womb" (see also Job 10:11). In Isaiah 66:9, God is a midwife who delivers children. God is a teacher in Isaiah 30:20 (see also Psalm 25:4-5).

5. *Objects people have made.* God is fortress, shield, horn, lamp, fountain, dwelling. In Psalm 119:114-117, God is "my hiding place and my shield . . . that I may be safe." God is "a sun and shield; he bestows favor and honor" (Psalm 84:11). In these cases an object, which has no life, is used to speak of a living and active God in relationship.

6. *The human body, mind, and emotions, with associated activities.* Images of God from this category are very common: God speaks, makes, thinks, plans, grieves (Ephesians 4:30), is angry (Romans 1:18), rejoices (Luke 15:7), changes his mind (Exodus 32:14), is jealous (1 Corinthians 10:22), even whistles (Isaiah 7:18)!

These words speak of God as if God had a human body, mind, and emotions. So the Bible also speaks of God's ears, eyes, nostrils (Exodus 15:8), arms, bosom (Isaiah 40:11), mouth, soul (Jeremiah 32:41), mind (Romans 11:34), fingers (Luke 11:20), gray hair (Daniel 7:9), even intestines (Isaiah 63:15— what the NRSV translates as "heart" is more literally translated as "intestines").

The word scholars use to refer to this kind of language for God is *anthropomorphism*—giving human characteristics to that which is not human, in this case, God. When Genesis 1:26-27 states that male and female are created in the image and likeness of God, it means that we are like God in some respects and not like God in other respects. Isaiah 31:3 denies that God has a body of flesh, and Hosea 11:9 states that God is not a human being, so these metaphors are not used literally. We are not to think of God as one who actually has arms and fingers—or even gray hair!

How, then, should we understand this language? These words do reveal something about God; they tell us about God and how God relates to the world. They are not to be dismissed as naive thinking. But, as with all metaphors, we need to ask where the point of comparison lies and how they are like (and unlike) God.

Most basically, giving God human characteristics reveals a God who is living and personal, who communicates with us and who interacts with us. Moreover, they reveal a God who is down-to-earth and close to our everyday experiences. The metaphors used for God are not religious or heavenly or dramatic. Go back through the list above. They come from everyday life—home and work, family and friends, fields and flocks, city and country, and especially personal relationships. Human beings, with all of our capacity for relationships, are believed to be the most revealing image of God in the life of our world.

There is a direct line between this kind of language for God and God's becoming flesh in Jesus Christ, "the image of the invisible God" (Colossians 1:15). In this human being God reveals to us most supremely who God is, how God relates to us and the world, and the depths to which God will go for our salvation.

What about God's eyes and ears? The Bible is not content with saying that God sees and hears us. By using parts of the human body, the Bible makes God's seeing and hearing more concrete and vivid. God's experience of the world, including you and me, is not superficial; God is close at hand and really sees. God "takes it in" in as real a way as do people who use their eyes and ears. At the same time, God "takes it in" in a way we do not— God takes it all in (Jeremiah 32:19), and not with eyes of flesh (Job 10:4). In Jesus Christ, God's eyes and ears do become flesh and reveal the lengths to which God will go to see us and hear us and save us.

So how might we answer the question in the title of this chapter? Yes and no!

Discussion Questions

1. Does God have eyes and ears? Explain your answer.

2. How is it important that the Bible uses relationship language to describe God?

12

What about the Book of Jonah?

IT IS OFTEN SAID that God must love stories because the Bible tells so many of them. Jesus must have loved stories, too, for he often speaks in parables. Stories are some of the most familiar parts of the Bible to us. You probably could retell the stories of the good Samaritan and the prodigal son from memory. Stories have a way of sticking in our minds and shaping how we think and act.

The stories Jesus told speak the truth, even though they are "made up," even though they did not actually happen. When Jesus made up the parables, he used his imagination and his rich knowledge of God and human beings to speak the truth. Truth can be conveyed through any type of literature, even fiction.

In chapter 8 we noted that readers of the Bible often are not told what type of literature they are reading. Recall the story about the vineyard in Isaiah 5:1-7, or Nathan's story about the lamb and King David in 2 Samuel 12:1-6.

We have a comparable problem with the book of Jonah. For more than 1,500 years scholars have disagreed about the type of literature that Jonah is. Some interpreters consider it a report of events in the life of the prophet named Jonah. Others consider it a parable like Nathan's story, or an allegory like Isaiah 5:1-7. Still others speak of Jonah as historical fiction, having some basis in fact but with much imagination used in telling the story. Regardless of the decision you make about this question, the book of Jonah speaks the truth about God and about God's relationship to people.

What evidence is available that may help us determine the type of literature that Jonah is? The verse 2 Kings 14:25 makes reference to a prophet named Jonah who announces good news to an undeserving Israel in the eighth century B.C. The book of Jonah likely has this prophet in mind. Yet no mention is made in 2 Kings that Jonah traveled to Nineveh, the capital of the Assyrian empire (the most violent of the empires of that time). It could be that the book of Jonah reports such a journey. At the same time, we know that Jewish authors used historical figures as a basis for speaking the truth through an imaginative story (historical fiction). Examples of this are the additions to the books of Esther and Daniel in the Roman Catholic Old Testament (see chapter 3). Is the book of Jonah another such example? We cannot be certain.

Jesus refers to Jonah in Matthew 12:39-41. Did Jesus think that the book of Jonah was a report of actual events? We cannot be certain. Jesus may have referred to Jonah in much the same way that you might refer to the good Samaritan as an example of showing mercy to those who need it.

The references in Jonah to extraordinary events are another factor to consider. Being swallowed by a fish and living to tell about it after three days in the fish's stomach is only one such reference. One has to be careful here to consider the possibility of miracle. At the same time, we must beware of making a jump from what God *could* have done to what God actually did do.

Other extraordinary features of the Jonah story may help us better understand the book: Jonah 3:8 states that even the animals of Nineveh fasted and cried out to God. Jonah 3:5-8 states that every person in Nineveh—a city with more than 120,000 children (4:11)—repented upon hearing Jonah's sermon. This would be a response without parallel in the history of preaching. Also, the size and population of Nineveh (3:3) are much larger than anything we know from archaeological excavations. It seems likely that these extraordinary features are examples of hyperbole, or purposeful exaggerations (see chapter 10). Hyperbole would be a fine way of emphasizing how even the worst of wicked people stand ready to respond to a witness to God.

Another factor to consider is the style of the book. Jonah is unlike any other prophetic book in the story form it takes. Notice also that the book ends with a question. This ending suggests that the book is not interested in reporting on events. Instead of being informed about what happened to Jonah, we as readers— who, like Jonah (4:2), often want to restrict the range of God's mercy—are confronted with a question to ask ourselves. Do we believe that God is ready to extend mercy to even the worst of sinners? Martin Luther noted that this way of ending the story is similar to the ending of Jesus' parable of the vineyard in Matthew 20:15 (Revised Standard Version): "Am I not allowed to do what I choose with what belongs to me? Or do you begrudge my generosity?"

So the book of Jonah, even if it is, say, historical fiction, speaks important truths about God and conveys to us an important message: God stands ready to be merciful to all the people of the world, no matter how deserving of punishment they may be. Even the prodigal son. Even you and me.

Discussion Questions

1. Discuss this statement: "Jesus' parables are fiction, yet they are true."

2. Given the discussion about the book of Jonah, what type of literature do you think that book is? Why?

13

Who Wrote the Bible?

WHO WROTE THE VARIOUS BOOKS of the Bible? Actually, this question is not as easy to answer as you might think. In many cases authors are unknown (for example, Judges, Kings, Hebrews). In some cases, names may be associated with books but for reasons other than authorship. For example, David is commonly called the author of Psalms, but the situation is far more complex (see the explanation later in this chapter).

And what do we mean by the word *author*? The word may mean that the content of a book originated in the mind of a single individual. But we use *author* in several other ways. For example, we know that presidential addresses often are composed by speech writers, celebrity autobiographies often are written by ghost writers, and students often use the ideas of other people in their term papers (sometimes using footnotes, sometimes without realizing it).

People in biblical times also had a broad understanding of authorship. For example, the writers of biblical books often used other sources. Sometimes they give a kind of footnote reference (see, for example, Numbers 21:14; 1 Kings 11:41). At other times, they don't. Chronicles uses Samuel and Kings as a major source (compare 2 Chronicles 6:32-33 with 1 Kings 8:41-43); Matthew and Luke use Mark (compare Matthew 15:32-38 with Mark 8:1-9).

Another example: Books sometimes are associated with people famous for a certain type of literature, though they may not be the authors of everything within them. David is associated with psalms, and Moses with laws.

Take Solomon. King Solomon, known for his songs and proverbs (1 Kings 4:29-34), is associated with several books of "wisdom," including Proverbs (1:1), Song of Solomon (1:1), and Ecclesiastes (1:1). On the basis of language and content, most scholars think that Solomon was not the "author" of these books, at least in the traditional sense. Perhaps words of Solomon were handed down over the years and then wise sayings were added from time to time, as Proverbs 22:17, 24:23, 30:1, and 31:1 suggest.

Take David. About half of the book of Psalms is associated with David (73 psalms, to be exact). Names associated with other psalms include Moses (90), Solomon (72, 127), Asaph (73–83), the sons of Korah (42–49), and others. We cannot know for certain whether the phrase "of David" (see Psalms 24–28) refers to authorship, or to literary influence, or to a collection of psalms associated with his name. About one-third of the psalms have no name attached to them. Psalms often were composed later than the time of David (for example, Psalm 137).

The linking of certain psalms to various individuals indicates that the book of Psalms in its present form consists of a collection of hymns and songs. Note also that the book of Psalms is divided into five smaller books (chapters 1–41, 42–72, 73–89, 90–106, and 107–150). This suggests that the book of Psalms is a collection, not only of individual psalms but also of smaller collections of psalms.

So the book of Psalms is similar to our modern hymnbooks, with compositions by various authors from various times collected into a single book. Other books may have been brought together in a similar way. It may be that some psalms originally were composed by women, as were other psalmlike texts in the Bible (for example, 1 Samuel 2:1-10, the song of Hannah).

This more complicated way of speaking of authorship in no way means that the books are any less inspired by the Holy Spirit. To use the language of Hebrews 1:1, "Long ago God spoke to our ancestors in many and various ways." Thanks be to God!

Discussion Questions

1. What are the difficulties in using the word *author* with biblical books?

2. Given the relationship between David and the Psalms, and Solomon and wisdom literature, how might you speak about Moses' relationship to the laws?

14

How Do You Read the Bible?

IN LUKE 10:26, JESUS ASKS a teacher of the law, "What is written in the law? How do you read it?" (New American Bible). *How* you read the Bible will affect what you read. Even more, how *you* read the Bible will affect what you read.

In the last several chapters, we explored some responses to the question of how to read the Bible. We have said that, as a reader, you need to consider such matters as the type of literature that a text is and the type of language used. For example, is the text prose or poetry? Are metaphors used?

As we learn how to read the Bible—it is a lifelong process—we also need to learn how to read ourselves. That is, when we read our Bibles we are not blank slates. We bring the people we are to the task of reading the Bible. Who we are will affect how we read the Bible!

WHO YOU ARE

Think for a moment about yourself as a reader of the Bible: man or woman, rural or urban or suburban, U.S. citizen or other nationality, ethnic roots, religious denomination, educational background, age, congregational history, economic status, and —especially—your own opinion about a variety of things. We all are deeply affected by what we have been taught and, more broadly, by the range of our life experiences.

Your interpretation of Bible passages will be shaped by the person you are. This is one basic reason why Christians have different understandings of Bible passages.

BLESSINGS AND DANGERS

The situation we have just described presents both blessings and dangers to Bible reading. One blessing is that we may more fully connect the Bible with our own lives and the lives of others. Our commitment to the Bible and to its witness to God may help us get inside the text more deeply and with greater insight.

One danger is that our own perspectives may overpower the text. We may end up listening to ourselves more than to the Bible. But there are some safeguards that we can put in place to help prevent this.

SIX SAFEGUARDS

1. Acknowledge the fact that you are bringing your own opinions to the text. Try to be alert to what these may be and how they may color your interpretation of Bible passages.

2. Make a clear distinction between the text and your own interpretation of the text. Whatever you say about a Bible passage is never the same as the Bible itself. Strictly speaking, the only words that should follow the phrase "the Bible says" is an actual quotation from the Bible in Hebrew or Greek.

3. Remember, therefore, that you are reading a translation of the Bible and that every translation is an interpretation, not an exact rendering. In previous chapters we have considered some of the reasons for differences among translations. Recall that one reason is that translators also bring their own perspectives to their work.

4. Remember that the Bible was written in times and places far removed from our own. Reading the Bible is a cross-cultural experience. We do have some things in common with people from Bible times; for example, we are human beings and we worship the same God. But we are quite different as well. We need to study what we can about the times in which the Bible was written, and that will help us to understand it better. Even so, we never can have a complete knowledge of that ancient setting in which the Bible was written.

5. It is important to listen to (or read about) the way others interpret the Bible. Especially helpful are group discussions of interpretations of individual passages. When we study the Bible together, we can share our interpretations and have our own readings of texts evaluated. Our readings may be corrected or enhanced, and we often will receive new insights from the way others read the text. This process can be even more helpful to us if we discuss our readings with people who differ from us.

6. Remember that Bible passages do not often (perhaps never) have a single meaning; texts are capable of meaning several things. The meanings we see in the text are a product of the interaction of three realities: the text itself, who you are as a reader, and the work of the Holy Spirit in the reading process. As you discuss passages with one another, several different meanings may emerge, all of which may be appropriate readings of the text. We will look at this more closely in the next few chapters.

Discussion Questions

1. In what ways is your reading of the Bible affected by who you are?

2. Discuss one or more of the "safeguards" and how they help you read the Bible.

15

Do Bible Passages Have More than One Meaning?

OVER THE YEARS, pastors will preach several different sermons on the same text. You may have heard two or more sermons on, say, Jesus' parable of the prodigal son. If you examined those sermons closely, you would see that the meaning of the parable changed somewhat (or a great deal!) from sermon to sermon. At the same time you probably would not suggest that only one of the sermons was true to the parable. It would be more truthful to say that the parable is rich enough to have several meanings.

Why does this parable, and other Bible texts, have several meanings? Remember what we said in the last chapter: "The meanings we see in the text are a product of the interaction of the text itself, who you are as a reader, and the work of the Holy Spirit in the reading process." Now let's take a closer look at these factors.

THE READER

The last chapter showed that who you are as a reader of the Bible affects the meaning you see in Bible passages. One reason the pastor's sermons change is that she is changing. She is gaining new knowledge and having new experiences. So every time she reads a Bible passage, she will see it with new eyes. This means that, to some extent, the pastor is involved in shaping the meaning of the text.

THE WORK OF THE HOLY SPIRIT

Another reason the pastor's sermons change is that God continues to work in her life. God weaves the pastor's ongoing experiences into the fabric of her faith, and new patterns in the text can be observed and new insights generated. God the Holy Spirit is not confined to just one meaning of Bible passages in order to speak to us. To insist on just one meaning for a text may restrict the work of the Spirit—as if the Spirit is at work only if we get the one "right" meaning. The Holy Spirit interacts with our spirit in such a way that Bible reading is a dynamic process and we are opened to new possibilities of meaning.

THE TEXT

Several factors are at work here:

1. New and different translations of the Bible generate new ways of thinking about texts.

2. Words often have different shades of meaning—in the original Greek or Hebrew, as well as in English. For example, my dictionary gives fifteen different meanings of the word *new*. New might suggest brand-new, redesigned, different, additional, unique, unheard of, advanced, or innovative.

3. Some words and phrases in the Bible invite you to use your imagination to discern meaning rather than to search for an exact definition. Take metaphors and similes (see chapter 10). For example, when the Bible speaks of God as father, you are encouraged to think about the lively world of parent-child relationships rather than just a precise meaning of the word *Father.*

4. Bible stories such as Jesus' parables invite you into an imaginative world. These texts encourage you to use your imagination as you reflect on that world. As you make these stories your own over time, their meaning becomes increasingly rich and gains ever-new depth and breadth.

THE MEANING OF BIBLICAL TEXTS

So, the meaning of the biblical texts is a "many-splendored thing." But, you may ask, does this mean that anything goes? No! A text cannot mean anything just because it can mean many things. The safeguards mentioned in the last chapter can help guide us here:

1. The text itself and the type of literature in the text.

2. The historical background information on such things as the people, events, and culture of the time when the text was produced.

3. The Christian community to which we belong and the confession of faith we make. The Gospel of Jesus Christ provides a center for our reading the Bible.

Reading the Bible is a creative activity in which something of the reader (that includes you!) becomes a part of the meaning of the text. Hence, Bible reading calls for your full engagement —through study, prayer, and openness to the work of the Holy Spirit in your thinking about the text. Recognition that texts are open to various meanings will foster more new insights, give more room for the play of the imagination, encourage conversation, and provide more avenues in and through which the Word of God can address people in our ever-diverse communities.

Think, for a moment, of a time when you were studying the Bible with others. Did everyone agree about the meaning of the text? Or the meanings in the leader guide? If there were different opinions, did you decide that only one was correct? Or, without suggesting that anything goes, did you let the differences stand and talk about them? If so, you were recognizing what we are saying here: Biblical texts have various meanings, and these can give you fuller insight into the truth about God and God's relationship to you.

Discussion Questions

1.   What factors affect how you read the Bible?

2.   What would you lose if you thought that the text had only one meaning?

16

Is the Old As New As the New?

Hᴏᴡ ᴡᴇʟʟ ᴅᴏ ʏᴏᴜ ᴋɴᴏᴡ your Old Testament? If you were asked to name favorite passages in it, what would you include? Perhaps Psalm 23; a few stories about Abraham, David, and Moses; and some texts in Handel's *Messiah,* such as "I know that my Redeemer lives" (Job 19:25). But if you are like most church people, you do not know your Old Testament very well.

Why? Because the church has tended to neglect the Old Testament compared with the New Testament. The Old Testament lesson may not always be read on Sundays (it is the first to go if extra time is needed). Pastors may seldom preach sermons on Old Testament texts. Many Christians are not as exposed to the Old Testament as they are to the New. For Protestants especially this is odd, especially considering that Martin Luther wrote so much about the Old Testament.

There are other reasons: Some people just don't like parts of the Old Testament. Christians often raise good questions about all the war and violence (see Deuteronomy 20:10-18), bloody animal sacrifices, prayers for vengeance on one's enemies (Psalm 137:7-9), or laws that seem irrelevant to modern life

(Deuteronomy 22:9-12; 23:19-20). These questions are not new. Christians have been raising them ever since the first century!

Part of the problem may be the word *old*. This word often means out-of-date or old-fashioned; most of us usually prefer the new. But *old* can be a good word, as in old cheese or aged beef or some wonderful old folks I know. Yet, because of this problem, some people have suggested changing the name of the Old Testament to Older Testament or First Testament or Hebrew Bible. But these suggestions have never caught on.

As we think about the place of the Old Testament in our faith and lives, it will be helpful to remember a few things:

1. The Old Testament was accepted as Scripture by Jesus and his disciples before the New Testament even existed. If the Old Testament was the Bible for Jesus, it certainly must be so for those of us who are his followers.

2. The Old Testament provides essential background for the New Testament. The basic teachings of Christianity are grounded in the Old Testament, including our understanding of God, of humans as both good and sinful, of faith and forgiveness, of judgment and grace, and of a strong concern for the poor.

3. The New Testament often quotes the Old Testament or alludes to it (more than 2,000 times!). By including the Old Testament so often in the New Testament, the Old becomes as new as the New. If one were to cut out the Old Testament, one would lose much of the New. This was demonstrated by a theologian named Marcion who tried to do just that (unsuccessfully) way back in the second century.

4. The Old Testament has spoken the Word of God to millions of people through the centuries. Many have heard from these pages God's word of comfort and forgiveness, indictment and judgment, encouragement and concern for our neighbor. To stand by the bed of a dying Christian and say the twenty-third Psalm together is to know that those "old" words have the capacity to speak deeply to Christians of every age.

5. The New Testament writers stake a claim about who Jesus is based on the Old Testament. Jesus Christ is the fulfillment of God's promises in the Old Testament. Without the Old Testament, Jesus may well be a good teacher and example, but he would not be the Messiah (or Christ). The Old Testament was essential for faith in Jesus as the Christ before there ever was a New Testament. If the Old Testament is set aside, the New Testament claims about Jesus based on it must be set aside as well.

It is true that Jesus helps us understand the Old Testament better. But it is equally true that the Old Testament helps us understand Jesus better. So let us be thankful that we have the Old Testament to help us know more fully what God is about in our world, most supremely in the person of Jesus Christ. And let us use it more often!

Discussion Questions

1. How would you define the words *old* and *new*?

2. Do you think that the Old Testament and the New Testament have equal value for your faith and life? Why or why not?

17

What Is a Prophet?

GO UP TO THE AVERAGE PERSON in the pew and ask for a brief definition of a prophet. Chances are you will get one of the two responses described below.

1. The prophet is a social reformer. People commonly use the word *prophetic* with this meaning. From this perspective, the prophet is an instrument of reform in Israel's society (and ours).

The Old Testament prophets do have much to say about the social, economic, political, and religious abuses of the times in which they lived. Isaiah 3:13-15 sounds a common note: "What do you mean by crushing my people, by grinding the face of the poor? says the Lord God of hosts" (v. 15). (See also Isaiah 5:8-9 and 10:1-3.) The prophets are very well-informed about these issues and speak a critical word from God about them. The prophets refuse to separate faith and the social problems of their time, particularly when they involve mistreating the poor and disadvantaged.

At the same time, to call the prophets simply social reformers is not enough. The prophets move beyond social analysis and put these abuses in relationship to God. The people's social and economic behavior show that their relationship with God is not right. In response, the basic word of the prophets is a call for repentance, not a social program. Yet the prophets also call for action on the far side of repentance, for it is remarkable how even those who repent can slip back into being abusive and neglectful.

In this call for social justice, the prophets appeal to traditional, conservative themes, particularly to those in the law of Moses (see Exodus 22:21-27). The prophets speak this old word into a new time and place in an especially forceful way. They show Christians the way to use the faith tradition to address social issues with passion and energy.

2. *The prophet is one who predicts the future.* The prophets do have many things to say about the future, especially words of judgment and promise. Because of sin, they speak of a coming judgment in this world—judgment that the people of God experienced at various times (for example, Jeremiah 4:19-31). But the prophets also speak promises. Those promises point to a coming One who will usher in a new age and rule as God himself would rule (for example, Isaiah 11:1-9).

At the same time, the word *predict* is not helpful. Words such as *announce* or *proclaim* would be better, for the prophets seldom were specific about the future of which they spoke. Regarding matters of time, for example, they often used inexact phrases, such as "in days to come" or "in that day" or "in those days" (Isaiah 2:2, 11; Jeremiah 3:18). In one of those rare cases when the prophet was precise (Jonah 3:4—"40 days"), he turned out to be wrong (Jonah 3:10)!

Moreover, the prophets' words about the future often consist of metaphors that cannot be tied down to a single, precise meaning. When Isaiah 40:4 promises that "every valley shall be lifted up, and every mountain and hill be made low," he is not suggesting that everything will look like Kansas or North Dakota!

3. Let me suggest this definition of a prophet: *A man or woman dispatched by God with a word of judgment or promise for a critical moment in the history of God's people.* The kind of word spoken by the prophet is shaped by the nature of that critical moment. What word from God do the people need to hear—then and now?

The prophets in the eighth and seventh centuries B.C. (for example, Amos, Hosea, Isaiah 1–39, and Jeremiah 1–25) most commonly indict the people for their sins and announce God's judgment. But after the fall of Jerusalem in 587 B.C., when the people were suffering in exile, the nature of the prophets' message changes. For such a time as this, the prophets bring words of comfort and hope (for example, Isaiah 40–55 and Jeremiah 30–33). Those who would use the words of the prophets today must discern the needs of this time carefully. What kind of word do we most need to hear today? Promises, yes, but we also may need some sharp words of judgment as well.

Discussion Questions

1. Without looking back at the chapter, how would you define a prophet?

2. Read Hosea 11:1-11. Do you find this inspiring or discouraging or both?

18

What Do the Prophets Say about the Future?

I AM AMAZED at how often the language of fatalism creeps into our thinking about the future. Someone has a close brush with death and says, "It wasn't my time to die." That thinking is not faith, it is fatalism. It is as though you could behave however you wanted because you won't die "before your time"!

Or take the matter of the environment. Some people say, "It doesn't make any difference what we do. The future is in God's hands; what we do about the environment is irrelevant." That attitude is a refusal to obey God's command to "have dominion" (Genesis 1:28).

Sometimes we speak of our personal futures in the same way. Some people think, "I won't take out insurance. I refuse to see a doctor. I won't prepare for my retirement. I will leave my future in God's hands." The devil tempted Jesus in a similar way, inviting Jesus to jump off the temple and have God's angels save him (Matthew 4:6). Jesus replied, "Do not put the Lord your God to the test." We should, of course, leave our future *ultimately* in God's hands. In the meantime, however, we are to take responsibility for our health and welfare.

Or, on a bigger scale, sometimes people try to figure out the time of the end of the world. The coming of the year 2000 has prompted some such speculation. Don't fall for it! Jesus clearly has said that we do not know when that time will come. "But about that day or hour no one knows, neither the angels in heaven, nor the Son, but only the Father" (Mark 13:32; also see Acts 1:7). Our only responsibility in such matters is to "keep alert" and trust God.

About these things the prophets may be of help to us. There is seldom a literal correspondence between the prophets' words and the future of which they speak. In the last chapter we spoke of their general language ("in that day") and their use of metaphor (see Luke 3:5). In Acts 2:17-21 Peter speaks of the coming of the Spirit as a fulfillment of Joel 2:28-32, but not literally (see verse 20). The prophets spoke of the future in ways that would speak to the people of their own time. When the "fullness of time" arrived, however, the fulfillment often took a form different from what the prophets had imagined.

This story might help us. A century ago a father made a promise to his young son: If he would maintain certain patterns of behavior, he would be given a horse and buggy on his twenty-first birthday. The years went by and the son followed his father's wishes. The time for the father to fulfill his promise was at hand. But in the meantime Henry Ford had been at work, and young men were then driving Model Ts. The only way in which the father truly could fulfill his promise to his son was to give him not a horse and buggy but an automobile. Had the father insisted on fulfilling the promise literally, it would have been no real fulfillment. Times had changed and so changed the way in which the father would remain true to his promise. So the father gave his son a Model T.

So it often is with the words of the prophets about the future. The fulfillment of God's promises in the coming of Jesus, for example, was more marvelous than anything the prophets imagined. It was so remarkable that many people in Jesus' time did not believe he was the fulfillment of the promises. Even Jesus' disciples had difficulty believing (see Luke 24:25). Only Jesus' careful interpretation of the Scriptures enabled them to make the connections (Luke 24:26-27, 32, 45).

We should not forget that it takes faith to discern that a prophecy has been fulfilled. We will not be able to figure it out by mathematical analysis. We walk by faith, not by sight. Prophecy is never a witness to itself, to its own ability to predict the future. Prophecy is a witness to God and God's faithfulness, which can be discerned only by a person of faith in a careful study of the Bible under the Spirit's guidance.

There may be people today who are studying the Bible and looking for a horse and buggy. They may miss the car!

Discussion Questions

1. Discuss the common understandings of the future that are outlined in the first three paragraphs of this chapter.

2. If someone told you that the world will come to an end on a certain date, how would you respond?

19

Can Prayers Shape the Future?

WILL A FUTURE EVENT come to pass if a prophet says it will? Not necessarily. Does what you say and do make a difference regarding the shape of your future? Yes.

Recall with me the story of Hezekiah in 2 Kings 20:1-7. Isaiah the prophet came to Hezekiah and told him, ". . . you shall die; you shall not recover." But Hezekiah understood that the prophet's words did not necessarily set his future in stone. And so he prayed. When God heard his prayer, God told the prophet to go back and tell Hezekiah, "I have heard your prayer, I have seen your tears; indeed, I will heal you." God was affected by Hezekiah's prayers. So much so that God changed the word of the prophet about his future. He would be healed.

But Isaiah was not satisfied with just the power of prayer. He commanded that a lump of figs (a poultice) be applied to Hezekiah's boil. Figs were thought to have healing capabilities in those days. The combination of prayer and the best available medical practice was effective in the healing process. God works to heal through both prayers and medicine.

Prayers can affect the future of communities as well as individuals. Remember how Moses' prayer affected the future of the sinful people in Exodus 32:11-14. In view of Moses' prayer, God "changed his mind" about the judgment! Hezekiah's prayers on behalf of the community also had this effect, according to Jeremiah 26:19.

Recall the story of Jonah. Jonah went to the city of Nineveh and announced, "'Forty days more, and Nineveh shall be overthrown!'" (Jonah 3:4). In response, the entire city prayed, fasted, and changed its ways. God, in turn, responded to what they did and "changed his mind about the calamity that he had said he would bring upon them; and he did not do it" (Jonah 3:10). What the prophet said about the future of Nineveh did not happen. God took into account what the people said and did, and their future turned out to be different from what the prophet had said it would be.

Read Jeremiah 22:1-5. God, through the prophet Jeremiah, commanded the people to act justly and take care of the oppressed and needy among them. Then God outlined two possible futures for them. If they obeyed this word, they would have a bright future. If they did not obey, they would experience great calamity. Their future depended on how they responded to God's word about justice and compassion.

We know from our own experience how true this is. How we treat our neighbors will shape our future, either positively or negatively. Note that God's future is affected as well. God will do different things depending on what the people do.

A story may help us understand. I used to play chess with my young daughters. When they were just learning, I knew that I could win the game whenever I wanted (though that changed in a hurry!). But the way in which the game would progress and the amount of time it would take depended on the various moves they made. As they became more skilled, the game became more complicated. I had to make different moves in view of theirs and that would change the progress of the game.

In some respects, our stories are like this. The future of our lives is somewhat open-ended. What we do and say—including our prayers—will shape our lives and the lives of others. God interacts with us, always working for our good and for the good of the world. But we can resist God's work by, say, neglecting the needy among us. God's decisions will be affected by what we do and say, and this will shape our futures.

And yet you will note that in none of these examples does God change his mind about promises of hope that the prophets speak. Though God's people made all sorts of complicated moves in their relationships with God, God kept his promises through thick and thin. God sent his son, Jesus Christ. God will keep his promises to us as well, even though we fail. Christ will come again and draw us into a new heaven and earth.

Discussion Questions

1. Discuss the prayers of Hezekiah and Moses and how they affected the shape of the future.

2. Your future is somewhat open-ended. Have you typically assumed that how you pray and how you assume your various tasks and responsibilities make a real difference?

20

How Does the Bible Have Authority?

W<small>HAT</small> <small>DO</small> <small>WE</small> <small>MEAN</small> when we say the Bible has "authority" for Christian faith and life? Many of us are suspicious of people in positions of authority these days. Polls show that we have less respect for our leaders, from politicians to clergy. Many people would claim that it is right to be suspicious; too many monsters have been let loose in the world by people in authority. The Bible often shares in this suspicion and loss of respect. Many people, even good church people, regard the Bible less highly these days than did their fathers and mothers.

There are many reasons for this situation. Let me list several matters for discussion that may help us think more clearly about the Bible's authority.

1. When we confess that the Bible is the Word of God, we refer to the Bible's unique capacity to speak God's word of judgment and grace to us. This word can bring life and salvation to individuals and communities.

2. Although the focus of the Bible's authority is this formational role, the Bible also is informational: It shows us what the essential content of the Christian faith was and still properly is. It identifies what the basic shape for Christian life in the world was and still properly is.

3. The Bible's authority is derived from the authority of God to whom it witnesses. For those who do not confess that the Bible's God is their Lord, the Bible is just one book among many.

4. People will see that the Bible has authority only when they see that "it works" for them—that it speaks to their daily needs and contributes to their well-being as individuals and to the building up of their communities.

5. Bible passages do not have authority for our faith and life in isolation from one another. Individual texts must be interpreted in the light of other biblical texts.

For example, biblical laws concerning slavery (Exodus 21) or the claim that "it is shameful for a woman to speak in church" (1 Corinthians 14:35) need to be examined in the light of the larger biblical message about freedom and equality. These examples show that the Bible does not have a single point of view about things. Hence, a certain amount of picking and choosing among texts is inevitable when speaking about what the Bible has to say about such issues. However, lively discussions among Bible readers who pick and choose differently help keep the Bible alive! These different points of view also help keep us humble. We never will get to the point when we can say, "Now I've got it all straight!"

6. Not every Bible passage has equal value for our faith and lives. For example, Psalm 23 has greater value than Paul's advice to Timothy that he take a little wine for the sake of his stomach (1 Timothy 5:23). Or the Ten Commandments have greater value than the command not to wear clothing of wool and linen woven together (Deuteronomy 22:11). It is not always easy to make such value judgments. But we are given some clues about how to do this by the fact that certain convictions (and not others) are drawn into creeds (for example, Exodus 34:6-7). The life, death, and resurrection of Jesus is a crucial centering matter for the task of interpreting all texts.

7.   The Bible does not have answers to all of our questions. The Bible writers were unaware of many of today's issues (for example, cloning, the age of the earth, birth control, the depletion of the ozone layer, euthanasia). What role the Bible should play in thinking about these matters is not always clear. We need to call upon wisdom that has been developed since Bible times to help us work through these issues. Truth about the world has been made available to us through fields of inquiry not directly related to the Bible or the church (for example, astronomy and physics).

Jesus promised us that he would send the Spirit to lead us into all the truth (John 16:13). This same Spirit also will help us see that we have not yet arrived!

Discussion Questions

1.   What do we mean by "the authority of the Bible"?

2.   The Bible does not have answers to all of our questions, so how are we to use the Bible when such questions arise? How have you found the Bible to be authoritative in your life?

21

How Is God Related to Suffering?

IN YOUR COMMUNITY, there is grief enough to freeze the blood. This ongoing experience of suffering has generated a variety of opinions. They include:

1.   All suffering is bad and to be avoided at all costs.

2.   All suffering is due to sin.

3.   All suffering is taking up the cross.

4.   All suffering is the will of God.

A close study of the Bible shows that none of these opinions is accurate. At the same time, it is difficult to say exactly what suffering is all about. At the least, we should think about different kinds of suffering. This chapter will explore this theme from five perspectives. No one of these perspectives, nor even all of them together, provides us with a definitive answer or explanation of suffering. But they may help bring us some insight into a reality that we will all experience at one time or another.

SUFFERING AS PART OF GOD'S GOOD CREATION

Some suffering is good and is a part of the world as God created it to be. We know from going to school that struggle and challenge are necessary for personal growth and development. In the world of sports and exercise, the phrase "no pain, no gain" rings true to us. As long as this kind of suffering contributes to life and well-being, it has a good purpose in God's creation.

Human beings are created with limits—of intelligence, agility, and strength. When we test those limits we may suffer, not because we sin but because we make mistakes. For example, when we slip or stumble we become subject to God's good law of gravity, and we may get hurt or even killed. God's good creation is not a risk-free place! Even before they sinned, Adam or Eve could have fallen from a tree and broken an arm, causing much pain. Sin could enter this picture if we stumble because, say, we are drunk or are pushed by someone.

From another angle, God has created a dynamic world, always on the move. Earthquakes, volcanoes, glaciers, and storms give ever new shape to God's good creation. Bacteria and viruses have their role to play in this "becoming" of the world. God does not micromanage these processes or plan them in some precise way. Rather God lets these aspects of the creation work as God created them to work. While this becoming of the creation is an orderly process in some basic ways, we must also speak of chance and randomness. What object a windstorm might pick up and where it might be blown is unpredictable. As Ecclesiastes 9:11 puts it, "time and chance happen to them all."

Because human beings are part of this interconnected world, we may get in the way of some of these processes in nature and get hurt by them. One thinks of the randomness of the gene pool, or tragic encounters with certain storms or viruses. We live in that kind of world! Sin could enter this picture if, for example, a habit of smoking cigarettes leads to harmful encounters with certain microorganisms.

SUFFERING AS THE CONSEQUENCE OF OUR OWN SIN

We know from experience that sins can cause suffering. If a person is reckless and drives a car into a wall, there will be suffering. We sometimes use the phrase "what goes around comes around," to describe these sorts of events. But such consequences do not happen because God pulls some kind of trigger when someone sins. Rather, they occur because God has made a world in which our actions have consequences. Such consequences are not inevitable, of course; the world does not work with that kind of precision.

SUFFERING AS THE CONSEQUENCE OF THE SINS OF OTHER PEOPLE

We often experience suffering not because of something we have done but because of what others have done to us. When the Israelites were in bondage in Egypt, they were suffering because of the sins of the Egyptians. Their suffering was obviously not the will of God; rather, God moved to get them out of the situation (Exodus 3:7-10). "Salvation" (Exodus 15:2) was God taking them out of the oppressive situation. We must remember that Jesus died not just to save us from our sins but to heal us from our hurt and from other ill effects of the sins of others.

SUFFERING AS PART OF BELONGING TO FALLEN COMMUNITIES

We also suffer because we belong to various communities that have had a long history of sinfulness and evil. Sin has become so pervasive that it takes on a life of its own and becomes a part of the very structures of our life together (family, town, nation, even congregations). Words such as ageism, racism, and sexism refer to this reality. We will be caught up in these effects on our communities, and we will make our own contribution to the suffering that coming generations experience.

SUFFERING AS A VOCATION

Suffering is sometimes associated with the vocation to which God calls us. Listen to 1 Peter 2:21: "For to this you have been called, because Christ also suffered for you, leaving you an example, so that you should follow in his steps." Suffering may come to us when we take up God's call to enter into the suffering of other people and make it our own. This is suffering that we could avoid. This is the only type of suffering that can be considered "taking up the cross" (Mark 8:34), and it can clearly be called God's will for our lives for the sake of our neighbor (see Isaiah 53:10).

In considering these matters, we should remember that suffering is no stranger to God. God does not remain aloof toward our suffering or relate to us as a mechanic relates to a "sick" car, seeking to fix us from the outside. Rather, God has chosen to get inside our world and, like good and powerful medicine, heal it from within. The God of Israel who truly "knows our suffering" (Exodus 3:7) has entered deeply into our suffering world in Jesus Christ and made it his own. When sufferings do come our way—and come they will—this God whom we know in Jesus will hold us in his hands and never, ever let us go.

Discussion Questions

1.   How has your understanding of God and suffering changed over the years? What experiences influenced these changes?

2.   How has God healed suffering in your life?

22

How Is God
Connected to Violence?

THE BIBLE OFTEN SPEAKS OF VIOLENCE. The Bible does so because it speaks of life as it is really is, rather than paint rosy pictures that are unreal. Most of us know that violence has been common among human beings throughout the ages, and it hasn't been getting better. In fact, the twentieth century will go down as the most violent century ever. And so when the Bible speaks of violence it connects with life as we have experienced it. Wars are frequent and people and animals get killed in large numbers (for example, 2 Samuel 8); people become slaves and are oppressed for years (Exodus 1-5); women are raped by strangers and by family members (for example, Genesis 34; 2 Samuel 13).

What often causes difficulty for Bible readers is that God is often associated with violence in the Bible. This is the case in both the Old Testament and the New Testament, though certain Old Testament texts receive most of the attention. How we think about this link between God and violence is important for Christian faith and life. In this chapter we consider certain forms of ecological and military violence.

Most of us are not thoroughgoing pacifists, but hold to some form of "just war" theory. The killing during World War II, for example, was commonly considered necessary in order to overcome the evils of Hitler's regime. Yet, Israel's killing of women, children, and animals, as commanded by God in some biblical texts, turns our stomachs. We should not forget, however, that this sometimes happened in America's wars, too; witness the saturation bombing of Dresden.

GOD AND THE PLAGUES

The story of the ten plagues (Exodus 7-12) has often troubled Bible readers, especially the killing of the Egyptian firstborn in the tenth plague (Exodus 12:29-30). While no final "explanation" is possible, certain comments may be helpful in thinking these texts through.

When the people of Israel in Egypt grew in strength and numbers (Exodus 1:7), this was considered the fulfillment of God's blessing in creation (Genesis 1:28). When Pharaoh (a kind of ancient Hitler figure) pursued a policy of genocide against Israel, he was violating God's intentions in creation and God's promises to the chosen people. In the face of this threat, God could not remain inactive. To this end, God acted through Moses and the environment to deliver the people of God.

Pharaoh's anti-creation activity had ecological effects, as virtually every part of the world of nature is adversely affected in the plagues. This negative effect on nature is not unlike that which occurred for the cities of Sodom and Gomorrah (see Genesis 19) or in later Israel (see, for example, Hosea 4:1-3). Sinful human behavior adversely affects the natural world, as we have learned so well in recent years. God does not bring these negative effects into being, but God mediates or "sees to" the consequences of these sinful actions so that sin and evil do not go unchecked in the world.

The plagues come to a climax in the tenth plague, the killing of the firstborn among the Egyptians. This plague should not be understood as God attacking the firstborn "in person." Rather, the text uses various Hebrew words in speaking of a non-divine agent that God uses, namely, an epidemic that kills quickly (Exodus 9:15; 11:1; 12:13, 23); one of these words is used for the cattle plague in Exodus 9:3. The killing of the firstborn should not be understood literally, but instead as a way of saying that no household remained untouched (Exodus 12:30). As with the other plagues, the emphasis on the words "all, every, whole" (compare Exodus 12:29 with 9:25; 10:14-15) portrays an aspect of nature that has gone berserk.

Finally, it should be noted that these texts in Exodus have been written in view of later worship practice, which included symbolic and dramatic language of various sorts. The insertion of instructions for the celebration of the Passover liturgy before the tenth plague occurs (Exodus 12:1-28) strongly suggests that the story is written in view of this later practice. The way in which the story of the other nine plagues is told suggests that it, too, has been written in view of a later dramatic celebration of these events, rather than a literal description (see the discussion of hyperbole in chapter 10). This drama captures two essential points. One, human sinfulness has negative effects on the environment; this is the way God's creation functions. Two, God uses these events to save Israel and deliver the people of God from oppression and genocide.

GOD AND WAR

Regarding war, Deuteronomy 20:16-17 puts the issue squarely before us. God commands the people of Israel: "But in the cities of these peoples [Canaanites] that the Lord your God gives you for an inheritance, you shall save alive nothing that breathes, but you shall utterly destroy them." Israel carried out this command in various battles recorded in Joshua 6-11.

No satisfactory explanation of this Israelite practice is possible. Yet, certain considerations may help us understand this cruel waging of war.

1. God works in and through human beings to achieve God's purposes. One such purpose was the settling of the people of God in the land of Canaan.

2. God does not perfect human beings, with their foibles and flaws, before deciding to work with them. God works with what is available, including the institutions of society. Among such institutions in that ancient context were certain ways of waging war and other trappings of government. Violence will be associated with God's work in in the world because, to a greater or lesser degree, violence is characteristic of the people and institutions through whom that work is done. Thus, such work will always have mixed results and will be less than what would have happened had God chosen to act alone. Moreover, God does not necessarily confer a positive value on those means in and through which God works.

3. Human beings will never have a perfect perception of how they are to serve as God's instruments in the world. It is difficult for us to evaluate Israel's perceptions in that time and place, because our context is so different. Israel's perceptions were often expressed in terms of the direct speech of God. Inasmuch as this is a phenomenon rare in the New Testament and in the church through the centuries, should we understand that direct speech in less than literal terms? Israel may have put into direct divine speech understandings they had gained through study and reflection rather than an actual hearing of God's words. And they may not have fully understood.

4. Israel's rationale for waging wars against the Canaanites in the way they did was twofold. One, so that they would not be led astray by their seductive religious practices (Deuteronomy 7:1-5, 16; 20:18). Two, they understood themselves to be the instruments of divine judgment against Canaanite wickedness (Deuteronomy 9:4-5). In view of this special purpose, Israel was commanded by God to wage war against other nations in less severe terms (see Deuteronomy 20:10-14).

5. That God would stoop to become involved in such human cruelties as war is not a matter for despair, but of hope. God does not simply give people up to experience violence. God chooses to become involved in violence in order to bring about good purposes. This means that evil will not have the last word. In everything, including war, God seeks to accomplish loving purposes and thereby prevent an even greater evil.

By participating in our messy conflicts, God takes the road of suffering and death. Through such involvement, God absorbs the effects of sinful human efforts and thus suffers violence. Indeed, God may even be said to assume part of the blame for what happens, for a divine promise of land for Israel lies behind the whole affair. That God finally experiences violence in the death of Jesus on the cross demonstrates that God himself gets caught up in the death that many people, including children, have had to experience, not least the Canaanites and the Egyptians.

Discussion Questions

1. Reflect on the story of the plagues and their ecological implications.

2. Reflect on the issue of "God and war" and the association of God with violence. How have you come to understand God and violence?

23

Our Best Questions

In this final chapter, I draw together some things we've discussed in the previous chapters. Find a fuller discussion of the points in the chapters themselves. When you read the Bible, it is important to remember all of these things:

1. Who you are—including your religious heritage, education, ethnic background, life experiences, gender, and opinions about all sorts of things—will affect how you read the Bible and what you see in the Bible. When you make claims about what the Bible says, remember that you are giving your interpretation. And your interpretation will need to be tested in the wider Christian community.

2. The Bible is a collection of books written over the course of many centuries. These books were only gradually recognized to have authority for the faith and life of the people of God.

3. Not all Christian Bibles have the same number of books; some churches have more books in their Old Testament than do Lutherans.

4. You are reading a translation of the Bible, not the text in its original languages, and every translation is an interpretation, not an exact rendering.

5. The Bible was written in times and places far removed from our own; that ancient setting must always be taken into account. Reading the Bible is a cross-cultural experience.

6. The Bible contains different types of literature. There are stories and hymns, parables and laws, laments and letters. Always ask: "What type of literature am I reading now?" Your answer will affect how you read.

7. Not everything in the Bible is intended to be taken literally. For example, metaphors are common: God is a rock or a father; Jesus is the lamb of God; heaven will have streets of gold.

8. Not everything reported in the Bible actually happened. For example, Jesus' parables are fiction. Yet, they are true. Truth can be conveyed through any type of literature.

9. Bible passages are capable of meaning several things. We can see this most clearly in the use of metaphors. When the text calls God a father, no single meaning is available. Generally any meaning we see in the text is the product of the interaction among who we are as readers, the text itself, and the Holy Spirit working in and through our reading. As scary as it may sound, something of who we are will be a part of any meaning we see in the text. That is one reason why we should be prepared to receive constructive criticism about what we think we have read in the Bible.

10. The Old Testament is just as important for Christian faith and life as the New Testament, but it is not always easy to determine how the two testaments relate to each other.

11. We don't always know who wrote the books of the Bible, and the word *author* was as complicated in Bible times as it is today. The Holy Spirit used many and various ways to bring us the Bible we have today.

12. The books of the prophets are not easy to interpret, and we should use great care in interpreting what they have to say about the future.

13. When we confess that the Bible is the Word of God, we refer most basically to the Bible's unique capacity to speak God's word of judgment and grace to us. The Bible also shows us what the essential content of the Christian faith is, and the basic shape for Christian life. At the same time, individual Bible passages do not have authority for our faith and life in isolation from other passages. We are called to read a text in the light of its larger context.

Each Christian is called not only to read the Bible but to study it. In this task, we are called to be fully engaged, with all our minds as well as all our hearts and souls. In our reading we are called both to be open and to question. The Bible's fullest potential is realized when we bring our best questions to the study of it. The Bible is better prepared to handle the tough questions than are many of its readers. To engage in genuine conversation with the Bible is one key way in which the Holy Spirit can work through you to open your eyes to the truth about God and God's world. And you will be able to witness more powerfully to the faith we confess. May God bless you in your study of the Bible!

Discussion Questions

1. Why is it important for you to bring your best questions to your reading of the Bible?

2. When you say, "The Bible is the Word of God," what do you mean?

Tools for Bible Study

STUDY BIBLES

HarperCollins Study Bible, ed. by Wayne A. Meeks, New Revised Standard Version, 1993.

The New Oxford Annotated Bible, New Revised Standard Version, 1991.

Both of the above study Bibles include extensive footnotes, colored maps, and introductions to each biblical book. Editions that include the deutero-canonical books in Roman Catholic and Orthodox Bibles are also published. Various other study Bibles are available for different translations.

BIBLE DICTIONARY

HarperCollins Bible Dictionary, ed. by Paul J. Achtemeier, 1996. Several thousand articles about every person, place, and thing mentioned in the Bible. Studies of the major biblical themes and introductions to each biblical book are included.

BIBLE COMMENTARIES

HarperCollins Bible Commentary, ed. by J. Mays, 1999. A one-volume commentary on each book of the Bible.

Interpretation Series, Westminster John Knox Press, 1982-present. This multi-volume series (usually one volume per biblical book) is very popular. For pastors and laity.

Westminster Bible Companion, Westminster John Knox Press, 1996-present. Only a few volumes of this multi-volume work especially designed for the lay person have been published at this point.

BIBLE INTRODUCTIONS AND STUDY GUIDES

Diane L. Jacobson and Robert Kysar, *A Beginner's Guide to the Books of the Bible.* Augsburg Fortress, 1991. Provides an introduction to each biblical book.

Craig R. Koeste, *Beginners' Guide to Reading the Bible,* Augsburg, 1991. A resource for further study of many of the questions raised in this book.